No One Can See the Hidden Ocean I've Created

826NYC BOOKS
372 FIFTH AVENUE
BROOKLYN, NY 11215

NO ONE CAN SEE THE HIDDEN OCEAN I'VE CREATED: POEMS BY 826NYC STUDENTS AT ACADEMY FOR YOUNG WRITERS © 2021 BY 826NYC AND THE AUTHORS. ALL RIGHTS RESERVED, INCLUDING THE RIGHT OF REPRODUCTION IN WHOLE OR IN PART IN ANY FORM.

FIRST 826NYC EDITION JUNE 2021

MANUFACTURED IN THE UNITED STATES OF BROOKLYN

978-1-948644-78-5

THE WRITING IN THIS BOOK WAS PRODUCED IN THE 2020-2021 SCHOOL YEAR AT 826NYC'S YOUNG WRITERS PUBLISH PROJECT AT ACADEMY FOR YOUNG WRITERS. THE CLASSES WERE RUN BY WILLIE FILKOWSKI WITH THE SUPPORT OF HENYA LA NOUE AND DEBORAH BARTON.

DESIGNED BY JOE IOVINO AND ANTHONY IOVINO

EDITED AND PROOFREAD BY MELISSA FEINMAN, JEN HA, MICHELLE HASKA, AMY LINSTROM, CHRISTINE MARELLA, LAUREN PRUITT, ALLISON SINGER, AND RACHEL SPURRIER

PRINTED BY BOOKMOBILE

THIS PROGRAM IS SUPPORTED, IN PART, BY PUBLIC FUNDS FROM THE NEW YORK CITY DEPARTMENT OF CULTURAL AFFAIRS IN PARTNERSHIP WITH THE CITY COUNCIL, THE JANE FRIEDMAN ANSPACH FAMILY FOUNDATION, THE HAWKINS FOUNDATION, THE RONA JAFFE FOUNDATION, THE KETTERING FOUNDATION, THE MINERVA FOUNDATION, THE PINKERTON FOUNDATION, AND THE RESNICK FAMILY FOUNDATION. THE PROGRAM IS ALSO MADE POSSIBLE BY THE NEW YORK STATE COUNCIL ON THE ARTS WITH THE SUPPORT OF GOVERNOR ANDREW M. CUOMO AND THE NEW YORK STATE LEGISLATURE. ADDITIONAL SUPPORT COMES FROM THE NATIONAL ENDOWMENT FOR THE ARTS. TO FIND OUT MORE ABOUT HOW NATIONAL ENDOWMENT FOR THE ARTS GRANTS IMPACT INDIVIDUALS AND COMMUNITIES, VISIT WWW.ARTS.GOV. 826NYC IS GRATEFUL TO THE MANY INDIVIDUALS WHO SUPPORT OUR WORK. TO SEE OUR FULL LIST OF SUPPORTERS OR MAKE A DONATION, PLEASE VISIT HTTPS://826NYC.ORG/DONATE-US/.

826NYC IS A NONPROFIT ORGANIZATION DEDICATED TO SUPPORTING STUDENTS AGES SIX TO EIGHTEEN WITH THEIR CREATIVE AND EXPOSITORY WRITING SKILLS AND TO HELPING TEACHERS INSPIRE THEIR STUDENTS TO WRITE. OUR SERVICES ARE STRUCTURED AROUND OUR BELIEF THAT GREAT LEAPS IN LEARNING CAN HAPPEN WITH ONE-ON-ONE ATTENTION AND THAT STRONG WRITING SKILLS ARE FUNDAMENTAL TO FUTURE SUCCESS.

Table of Contents

David Areche   8
   Determined and Daring to Dream
   A Chaotic Caring Combo

Tameyah Argudin   10
   The Good Ol' Reliable
   How the "Good Ol' Reliable" Tameyah Came to Be

Ciara Ayala   14
   Strong & Brave
   The Impossible

Ciara Camilus   16
   The Person Behind the Simple Expression
   The Vision

Chloe Campbell   18
   My Hungry Disposition
   The Faithful Roots of Rain

Makayla Campbell   20
   A Different Fairytale
   I am From Brooklyn, New York

Arianna Crews   22
   One Word Can Change It All.
   The Love Is Real.

Damaris Cruz   25
   I Am Someone... Just Don't Know Who

Akoni Drysdale-Ash   26
   I Am Poem
   Where I'm From Poem

Jaynise Duval — 29
    I Am Strong and Focused

Alexandra Flores — 30
    Present in Front, Past Lingering
    Places Far Away

Licia Garcia — 32
    A Descriptive Perspective
        of a Person With Strong Feelings
    A True Emotion of a Person With Hard Feelings

Cassidy Grays-Ferguson — 34
    The Life I Live
    A Day and a Life of Cassidy Ferguson

Sadeyah Harrison — 36
    The Girl Of Your Dreams.
    Fear Is The Biggest Battle
    That Place With All the Kids

Richelle Ashanti Horsford — 40
    I Am Who I'm Supposed To Be
    Peace in the Streets

Brianna Jackson — 43
    i am poem

Khalik Johnson — 44
    I am Greatness
    I survived Brooklyn NY

Shanice Jackson — 46
    I Am poem
    Backstage

Aries Jones   49
    The Poisonous Snake~

Thomas Jones   50
    I am poem
    I am from poem

Robert Kearney   53
    I Am Poem

Sherebiah Lawes   54
    A Game of Chess with One Million Pieces on the Table
    Powerfully broken

Malaki Lesser   58
    What My Life Poem
    My Goofy Poem

Diani Lucas   60
    That's So Diani
    The Life of Ms. Lucas

Jamel Mayo, Jr.   62
    I Am Poem
    Where I Am From

Schnieder Milien   65
    Happiness

Leshaun Miller   66
    The World is an Unforgiving and Generous Place
    The place I belong

Dionyae Mitchell   70
    This is Me
    The Birth of Me

Lillian Olivari 72
    I Am from the Love of My Family
    I Am Who I Pretend to Be

William Perez, Jr. 76
    Positivity
    I Am Family.

Sa´Nye Seabrook 78
    Wish it, Want it, Do it
    The Truth Behind the Happiness.

Nathaniel Stewart 80
    The Beginning of the End
    Behind The Skin

Celina Torruella 82
    I am Celina
    I am from Home

Kamani West 84
    The Blessing in Disguise
    The Quiet Face Behind It All

Skyla W. 86
    Can You See Me
    Can you see past the cover

ABOUT THE AUTHORS 88

ACKNOWLEDGEMENTS 102

ABOUT 826NYC 104

Determined and Daring to Dream

by David Areche

I am nice and kind
I wonder if I'm going to be successful in the future
I hear the wind
I see myself being something good in the future
I want to be in the NBA

I pretend to be like no one
I feel somebody walk past me
I touch my pet fish Nemo
I worry about something bad happening to me
I cry about stuff sometimes
I am smart and funny

I understand that I'm not perfect
I say that I will be something good in the future
I dream that I will be an NBA player
I try my best in everything I do
I hope that nothing goes downhill for me
I am determined and hardworking

A Chaotic Caring Combo

by David Areche

I am from my enormous living room

From coconut oil shampoo and conditioner

I am from my messy bedroom with shoes all over the place and my bathroom that smells of flowers

I'm from my kitchen where I can taste my grandmother's delicious lasagna

I am from the smell of Febreeze

The red rose plant I have

The trees outside my home

I am from the beautiful dance of salsa and curly hair

I am from Angellica and Socrates

I am from an attitude problem family and a lot of gossiping

I am from my grandma telling me to "Do your homework" and "Who you talking to like that"

I'm from listening to "Twinkle twinkle little star" and "Rain rain go away"

I am from Thanksgiving

I am from Philadelphia, Pennsylvania and my parents are from Dominican Republic and Ecuador

I am from arroz con pollo y habichuelas

From my grandma telling a lot of horror stories since she was a kid

From album photos and picture frames around my house

The Good Ol' Reliable

by Tameyah Argudin

I am reliable and driven.
I wonder if I'll have a completely different persona when I grow up.
I hear my best friend and I gossiping over some boiling hot tea that we got from social media.
I see my old self congratulating and cheering me on for my achievements.
I want to make my family proud.
I am reliable and driven.

I pretend that I'm in a perfect daydream consisting of purple and pink clouds, magical creatures, and some R&B music.
I feel for the people who have less than me.
I touch the mental scars that were left behind in my head to remind myself of where I came from and where I am now.
I worry about how I'll turn out in the future.
I cry when I get stressed over things that aren't in my power to control.
I am reliable and driven.

I understand that life isn't easy.
I say keep on going, it's going to be worth it in the end.
I dream for a world with peace.
I try to keep my feelings in check, but sometimes I struggle with them.
I hope that the world gets better.
I am reliable and driven.

How the "Good Ol' Reliable" Tameyah Came to Be

by Tameyah Argudin

I am from a bunch of clothes, whether it's from laundry or a recent shopping spree, and from the music on Sundays telling my family to get up and clean.

I am from the noisiest but connected household, from the lavender Fabuloso that you smell after us cleaning the house.

I am from the cherry blossom trees that grow in the spring in my neighborhood,

the cherry blossom trees' petals that always leave their mark on the sidewalk.

I'm from the annual 4th of July barbecues that my Aunt throws

and the funny jokes that are always being thrown at others

and from my ever-so-curious grandmother and my blunt mother.

I'm from the loud music that you hear when someone's in the shower and hearing everyone's phone conversation once they start walking around the house

and the ganging up on a family member once they do something idiotic.

I'm from being told that turning on lights in the car will get us pulled over by the police and the "I'll give you something to cry about" threats when I'm crying and the old-school music you'll eventually learn once hearing them on too many "cleaning Sundays".

I'm from the birthday parties that always start and end with a bang.

I'm from Brookdale Hospital due to myself being too eager to enter the world and the Cuban in me from my father's side and the fried chicken and baked mac & cheese that my mom makes.

From my uncle getting his leg burned by being too close to a firecracker, he was always the crazy uncle, to the family portrait we took for my mom's graduation that's hanging up in the living room.

I am from one crazy family, yet the best family I could ever ask for.

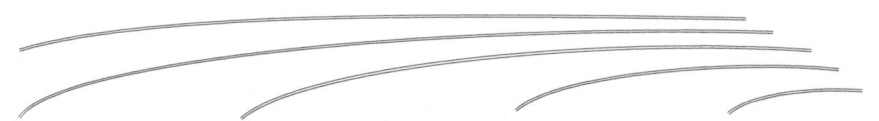

Strong & Brave

by Ciara Ayala

I am strong and brave

I wonder how did what I do

I hear water

I see butterflies, and a light

I want my dad back

I am strong and brave

I pretend I am happy and okay but really I'm hurt

I feel my dad holding me

I touch my dad's hand

I cry because I miss him so much

I am strong and brave

I understand he is gone and not coming back

I say life will not be the same without you

    but I will be fine

I dream that I can see you again

I try to keep mom happy and not depressed

I hope one day we will have something

    we dreamed and wanted

I am strong and brave

The Impossible

by Ciara Ayala

I am from the quiet house
from the blankets and pillows
The yellow red and brown house
from in the cozy rooms
I am from the beds
The big tall tree outside

I'm from big parties and screaming

From my grandma and grandpa

I'm from the headaches and loud music

And from always shopping

I'm from being very crazy and loud

And "be nice"

I'm from the cooking

I'm from Brookdale hospital and Puerto Rico

Empanadas and pastelles

From my auntie passing away so young

her fighting cancer at the beginning of the year to passing away at the end

The photos books

From the boxes of photos and cameras with videos

The Person Behind the Simple Expression

by Ciara Camilus

I am from phones

From headphones and chargers

from the constant chaos

and awkward tension

The bewitching cherry blossom tree

Who is now long gone but forever remembered.

I'm from yearly summer camping trips and rowdy relatives

from Katherine and Kayla

I'm from insensitivity and prying

and from bluntness

I'm from "you can't because you are a girl..." and dress codes

and "Girlfriend" by Avril Lavigne

I'm from New York City and Haiti

Bannann Peze and Griot

From the time my sister broke her arm when climbing the monkey bars.

Distressed cries, stinging pain, and constant hospital visits.

The Vision

by Ciara Camilus

I am me.

I wonder where I'll be in the years to come.

I hear my fate.

I see my destiny.

I want to find true happiness.

I am me.

I pretend that I am someone else.

I feel my worth.

I touch my benefit.

I worry for my future self.

I cry, but why?

I am me.

I understand the world's twisted games.

I say I am better.

I dream of success.

I try to make my dreams a reality

I hope to find pure happiness.

I am me.

My Hungry Disposition
by Chloe Campbell

I am smart and quiet

I am forever hungry and smart

I wonder what I should eat when I get home

I hear some music and it's so-so

I see school girls hitting the woah

I want Popeye's but they're too slow

I am forever hungry and smart

I pretend I'm full when I could go for another bite

I feel so warm like I have touched the light

I touch my stomach and had a small fright

I worry there is no more food

I cry because my worry came true

I am forever hungry and smart

I understand that I exaggerate

I say "Give me my meal, with no malice or hate"

I dream about my love of food

I try to share that dream, but with whom?

I hope to diet but that's a stretch

I try to eat salads but I can only wretch

I am forever hungry and smart

The Faithful Roots of Rain

by Chloe Campbell

I am from the refrigerator
From face wash and Dove Sensitive Skin
I have rooms, a kitchen and bathrooms.
I am from the feel of carpets
The aloe vera plant I have
The trees outside my home
The pollens that chase me
Oh how I wish they'd leave me alone.

I am from the sunday feasts and the monday leftovers
From my often used pore strips and face masks
I'm from my mom and my dad
And from winter barrels

I am from the "sitting too close the TV screen is bad for you"
And "Carrots are good for your eyes"
And "never say never"
And from summer shopping in winter
I'm from America and Jamaica at the same time
Stewed peas and various soups
From my mom falling out of a tree when she was a kid
She never got hurt though!
From photo albums
And photos of my family on the wall

A Different Fairytale
by Makayla Campbell

I am silly and smart

I wonder what I'll be when I grow up

I hear the mermaids sing

I want amazing grades

I am pretty and smart

I pretend I'm a mean person

I feel Tinkerbell's shoes

I touch Captain Hook's hat

I worry about reality

I cry about my grades

I am silly and smart

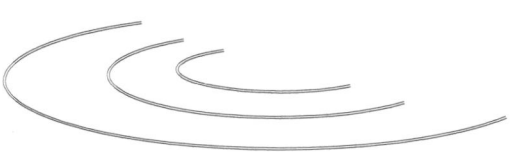

I understand my love for music

I say getting something without working for it is unrewarding

I dream to be flawless and intelligent as the beauty standard for today's society

I try to be perfect for everyone else

I hope life gets better

I am silly and smart

I Am From Brooklyn, New York

by Makayla Campbell

I am from Brooklyn, New York
where they shoot at the sky with broken dreams
    from fake gangsters,
where on fourth of July they shoot up the streets
    not with guns
just illegal fireworks
and the cops chase them around cars as we record and laugh
when we go to the beach
and play ball with strangers amazing good memories getting
    stuck in traffic
due to protests against the police and gun violence
and all we can do is pray it gets better

People always say take a little bitter with the sweet
So we must take all this bitter horrible crime and mix it with
    all the amazing things we cherish
like the malls
All of our tourists spots and amazing places to pick up food
Even though our crime rate is through the roof
We are the best place to come for a nice tourist if it comes
    down to the amazing tourist spots

We are a tourist spot already,
The Statue of Liberty, Central Park,
Empire State Building, Times Square, Brooklyn Bridge,
Fifth Avenue, New York Public Library,
Ice Cream Museum, Madame Tussaud's Wax Museum,
    and 29 Rooms
All good for Instagram in the craziest state
Even though the music is bomb and we have the best
    tourist spots
we still have our downsides just like every other state
but we are just better.

One Word Can Change It All.

by Arianna Crews

I am powerful and confident

I wonder if I walk outside if it's going to be my last step.

I hear my mother shouting for me to do the dishes.

I see people worried to go outside because of the violence.

I want the world to go back to normal.

I am powerful and confident

I pretend like I don't care, but I do.

I feel blessed every time I wake up in the morning, knowing I made it past another day.

I touch my mother's heart every time I do well.

I worry that it will soon be my last day with my grandmother.

I cry because I get stressed out.

I am powerful and confident

I understand I can't always have my way.

I say I'm going to keep pushing, but I give up sometimes.

I dream of a day without violence.

I try not to eat all the food in the house.

I hope I make it to college.

I am powerful and confident

The Love Is Real.

by Arianna Crews

I am from the building where they are always blasting music.

I am from an apartment that has the best cooking.

I am from a home with many animals.

I'm from a family where it's a heap of stones. Remove one, and the structure will collapse.

I'm from a family where they can be fudge but mostly sweet, with a few nuts.

I'm from a family where they are as loud as a siren.

I'm from a place where it's like a puzzle, sometimes you don't have all the pieces together or sometimes it all fits together at the end.

I'm from a place where it's like cooking, it can be all fun sometimes but the recipes might not go accordingly, you can mess up.

I'm from a place where life is also like a banana. It starts out green and firm, but it gets mushy with age. It's also a bit slippery from time to time, but everyone wants to stick together in the right bunch.

I'm from a place where my childhood was like a zoo but I was one of the animals. Always all over the place.

I'm from a place where someone always has to be scared to come outside because of the violence.

I'm from a place where kids have to grow up wearing masks because Covid.

I'm from a place where it's like a maze, you have to find your way through in order to survive. That's life.

I Am Someone...
Just Don't Know Who

by Damaris Cruz

I am trustworthy and hopeless
I wonder what my future looks like
I hear the next global problem getting ready to wipe us out
    because we thought we were safe
I see lifeless souls walking around with a mask
I want to be great I feel it's what I deserve
I am trustworthy and hopeless

I pretend I'm in another world where people value each other
    and respect each other
I feel like nothing will ever interest me in life
I touch my future as it crumbles in the palm of my hand
I worry about losing people I love
I cry when I have anger building inside of me with no
way to escape
I am trustworthy and hopeless

I understand I can't always get the things that I want
I say that I'll never trust anyone like I used to because people
    saw that and took advantage of it
I dream of my mother living in a big house with everything
    that she wants stress-free
I try to make those who see greatness in me happy
I hope this world is not too far gone
I am trustworthy and hopeless

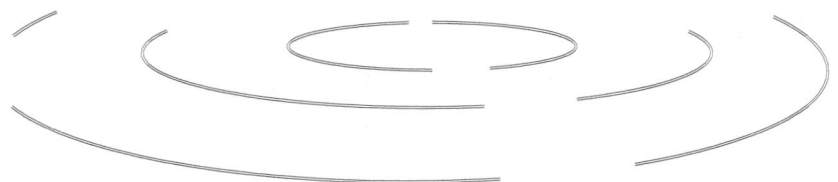

I Am Poem

by Akoni Drysdale-Ash

I am Manly and Weak

I wonder if I can make it to be successful

I hear all the Black lives lost and I hear revenge

I see protests I see tears I see fights

I want to save lives and avenge my dead ancestors

I am Manly and weak

I pretend I'm Happy

I feel my success I feel happiness coming

I touch the halfway mark there but around me is pain and defeat

I worry if I'll be happy and successful

I cry when I'm unhappy and when I feel alone

I am Manly and weak

I understand that I'll never be what I really wanna be

I say in my next life I'll be a male and that I'll be comfy

I dream to help the world and myself

I try to have better times and better days

I hope to be a better person

I am Manly and weak.

I pray my Grandma gets better

Peace and soul—Jaqueline Davis

Where I'm From Poem

by Akoni Drysdale-Ash

I am from My computer and My phone

From my TV and my TV remote

I am from the slums and the trenches

The smell of bacon eggs and cheese and a sunny project breeze

The coming back to life trees and grass

Whose long gone color and value is long gone but returns in spring.

I'm from vanilla-tasting pancakes and Family barbecues

From grandma and grandpa's house

I'm from becoming distant and reconnecting

and from our family bond resurrecting.

I'm from "you're not a boy" and "are you a boy or girl"

and from "you got a friend in me"

I'm from going to birthday parties and celebrating

I'm from Manhattan hospital and Trinidad and waffles with bacon

From you look like your great grandma

I am from pictures of my mom and my brothers and my cousin's house and my bedroom window.

I Am Strong and Focused

by Jaynise Duval

I am strong and focused
- I wonder about my future
- I hear the wind flowing
- I see a blue sky
- I want to live a good life

I am strong and focused

- I pretend I'm a hairstylist
- I feel someone is with me
- I touch the clouds above
- I worry about my family
- I cry when I'm depressed

I am strong and focused

- I understand why to stay inside
- I say I am strong and brave
- I dream about my future
- I try to be successful
- I hope to have a career

I am strong and focused

Present in Front, Past Lingering

by Alexandra Flores

I am from the books me and my sister have collected throughout all these years,
from all the hair products and hair ties that once kept it all tight.
I am from the the small apartment in a old and dirty building, the same buildings that line up the streets of Brooklyn
I am from all the plants my mother keeps inside this small place we call home,
from all of the nature we once used to grow
The big palm trees that were once outside my real home. The real trees whose long limbs I remember as if they were my own.

I'm from all the meals me and my family used to share among the dead among the living
From all my aunts, my mothers, my sisters and all the family we have and lost.
I'm from that need to be the best in life and from those lessons taught by their words and by this life and from every day she wasn't there and each day I didn't care

I'm from "Stop being a brat" and "Be careful." Those words build my base to make me the person I am today.
I'm from broken traditions I once held dear
I'm from the place of freedom where people are still locked in chains.
I am from all the Chicken, rice, beans, and salad you could possibly eat.
I am from every day I grow older and from every day I inch closer. Closer to being held in a casket. Closer to seeing their graves.
I am from all you can think of and more beyond these words.

Places Far Away

by Alexandra Flores

I am foolish yet alive.

I wonder why I live this life but when I hear my friends laughing I understand why.

I can see the ghost of my younger self smiling, Her face lighting up the darkness

that held me. I'm questioning and wondering why I am foolish yet alive.

I wish I was in the sky above. In the dark place we call space.

I can see myself floating in the loneliness and solitude of the dark sky.

I feel all the ghosts of my past and present laughing and dancing.

They looked so happy and yet I couldn't help myself from crying.

I cried for the dead or maybe it was for the feeling, I am foolish yet alive.

I know this world is cold, Colder than a knife but I'll keep living on because I am foolish yet alive.

I had dreamed of a world far away.

A world where I could be freed from this hellish place and yet night after night I fail to reach the heavenscape.

I hope and keep hoping for the day I will fly. But until then I am foolish yet alive.

A Descriptive Perspective of a Person With Strong Feelings

by Licia Garcia

I am poem.
I am shy and cute.
I wonder if I could ever sing on a stage without my anxiety from other people.
I hear my mother sing her sorrows away.
I see an image of my future life soon to play.
I want to be a better person for everyone who depends on me.
I am shy and cute.

I pretend I was in a different happier world where everybody will love me.
I feel a spirit's touch on me to protect me and other children from harm.
I touch my little sister's hand to hold it and keep her safe. (Yes, I'm the oldest child)
I worry all my favorite family loved ones will die soon.
I cry when someone insults me and makes me upset.
I am shy and cute.

I understand what many people go through every day.
I say that no matter what, don't let somebody tell you that you are different you are beautiful.
I dream of my old childhood memories every day.
I try to change and do better for myself, but I sink in my own guilt and stress.
I hope everybody that I love and trust is not upset about anything, about someone, or themself because I'm a positive person; I want you loved.
I am shy and cute.

A True Emotion of a Person With Hard Feelings

by Licia Garcia

Where am I from poem!

I am from a missing feather from my small bird and the window that blew wind

I am from the abandoned apartment called an apartment

I am from a sakura blossom

The tree that bloomed pink in every spring.

I'm from my dad's side and I look like my mother

from my mother and my father

I'm from eating and talking a lot to each other

and from learning to listen.

I'm from don't grow up too fast and don't expect everybody to be nice like you and live my life

I'm from having a nice dinner with the whole family

I'm from Brookdale Hospital and my mother's grandmother and father

And chicken and barbecue ribs

From when my grandmother had sadly passed away due to sleeping peacefully we had some pictures of us and her to share memories every day it was located in my mother's drawer where she kept thousands of her memories in! And in my heart as well.

The Life I Live

by Cassidy Grays-Ferguson

I am tired yet still trying
    I wonder if life will be the same again
    I hear life ain't easy
    I see big things ahead of me
    I want COVID to be over
I am tired yet still trying

    I pretend that everything is good
    I feel like things are not the same
    I touch the clouds above
    I worry I'll die
    I cry when I feel like I'll die
I am tired yet still trying

    I understand that things get hard
    I say that I will make it
    I dream to get out of school
    I try to make it
    I hope to have a nice future
I am tired yet still trying

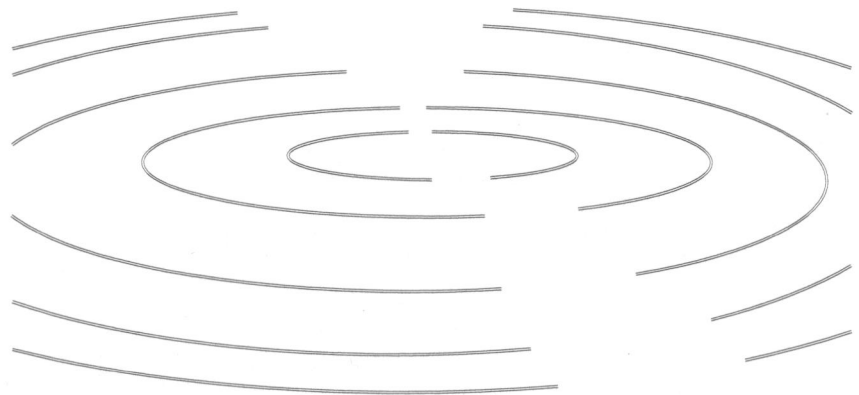

A Day and a Life of Cassidy Ferguson

by Cassidy Grays-Ferguson

i am from waking up to two dogs outside my room door from dogs barking and people yelling

i am from the hood where it smells like cigarettes and weed outside my house

i am from leaving my house every other day and going to my grandmother's house from drunk and high family members

i am from uncles getting locked up and having them in and out of jail and from people in and out of my grandmother's house

i am from people saying you won't make it in life and look at me now and never trust nobody everyone is not your friend

i am from family not getting along

i am from the bronx and new york city

and fried chicken and rice from my grandmother getting hit by a car in front of my face like we were walking across the street and my grandmother moved me and my older sister out of the way so we wouldn't get hit and she tried to make it across but she didn't.

The Girl Of Your Dreams.

by Sadeyah Harrison

I am smart and talented.

I wonder if I'm making my family proud

I hear all the negativity rarely the positive on the news,

I see people needing help, I barely see others helping

I want a change,

I am smart and talented.

I pretend to be happy at my lowest,

I feel the anger boiling inside,

I touch others' hearts so they can be happy,

I worry, is that the right thing? do I come first?

I cry in silence I stand tall,

I pretend to be happy at the lowest

I understand my worth and what I deserve,

I say I do understand,

I for the better, I try to make changes,

I hope this violence and hurt comes to an end,

I understand my worth and what I deserve.

I am smart and talented.

Fear Is The Biggest Battle

by Sadeyah Harrison

I am from a cold place where people have a sad story,

It makes you wanna stay home, isolate, and just imagine yourself somewhere that's totally different,

For this you just look at people and say wow look at them and look at me you will feel like a superstar like you accomplished something,

I am from a place I have to watch my back every step I take,

I am from a place where people argue over childish things and end up killing each other,

I am from a place my little brothers can't even play in a park without them getting hurt,

I am from a place you can't be free at,

If you're free you're an animal you're so many things but yourself people move away from you make you feel like you're a wild gorilla on the loose you feel like a virus people are trying to kill,

I am from a place where the image is nice but deep down inside it's ugly

I am from New York

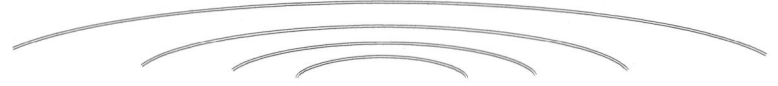

That Place With All the Kids
by Sadeyah Harrison

I am from a loud and funny home
I am from the best smelling and cleanest apartment
 In my building
I am from the home with the two dogs

I'm from America and a black home
I'm from a family with 10 kids in total
I'm from a stable home
I'm from a football family

I'm from an out of control class and a big school, so big you
 may need a map to walk around this maze you may think
 you're walking in a traumatic problem like a math
 word problem impossible to solve
I'm from hip hop and loud cursing for no reason music
I'm from sports

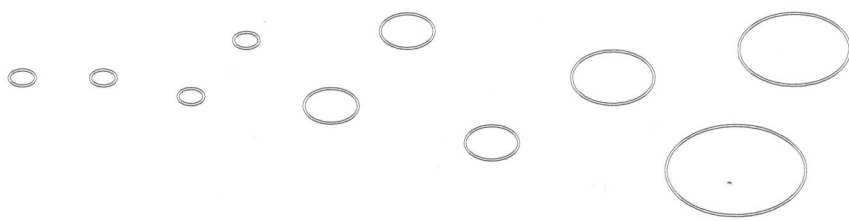

I Am Who I'm Supposed To Be

by Richelle Ashanti Horsford

I am sensitive and relaxed
I wonder if I let people get to me would I be the person I am
I hear the drama
I see the fights
I want to succeed
I am sensitive and relaxed

I pretend I'm famous
I feel the pressure
I worry that I will fail
I cry because I feel like I'm not good enough
I am sensitive and relaxed
I understand that I can't change people
I say the wrong things
I dream about the future
I try to change
I hope for the best
I am sensitive and relaxed

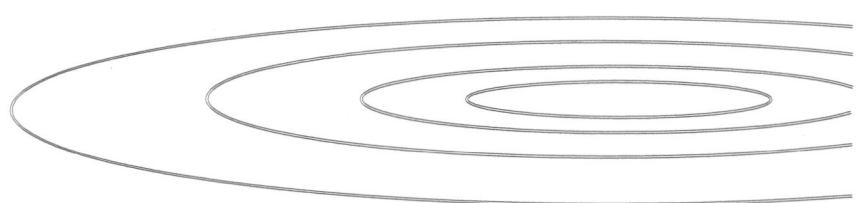

Peace in the Streets
by Richelle Ashanti Horsford

I am from two overprotective parents and four brothers
From a loud house but quiet neighborhood
I am from where everyone talks about everyone but acts like it never happened in the face
The tree where cats always find their way up and shockingly down too

I am from late-night hangouts and a mother who stops and talks to everyone
from we leaving in five minutes turning into we've been here for hours
I am from where everybody knows everybody and playing traffic in the alley was fun
and from cheating in cops and robbers by using vehicles when it was a no-vehicle game (that's where the trust issues started)

I am from getting back up and trying 'til I get it
and not everything is forever
I am from that park where my dad took me to watch the soccer games on Sundays
I am from bright lights and big buildings
Rice and peas and oxtails
From going to the hospital once a year because somebody's sick, baby pictures and stories of everybody's childhood, like when my uncle ate my grandmother's ice cream when he was a kid. That story never gets old, unlike the people. Paintings, pictures that all hold a special memory.
I am from the city that never sleeps, in Alicia Keys' words, "In New York, Concrete, Jungle, wet dream, tomato." Nah lemme be for real, "In New York, concrete jungle where dreams are made of."

i am poem
by Brianna Jackson

i am loved
    i am a sister
    i am joyful
    i feel unstoppable
i am loved

    i am smart
    i am brave
    i'm a dreamer
    i think everyone can't be trusted
i am loved

    i am black

I am Greatness
by Khalik Johnson

I am smart and young.
I wonder what I will become.
I hear high school calling my name.
I see my nice shiny sliver college building welcoming me in.
I want to get a good and nice education.
I am smart and young.

I pretend I am in the NBA.
I feel like the greatest.
I touch the NBA courts.
I worry that high school will be hard.
I am smart and young.

I understand school is very important.
I say that I want school to be over.
I dream that today could be faster.
I always try to do my best in school.
I hope that I pass the 8th grade.
I am smart and young.

I survived Brooklyn NY

by Khalik Johnson

I am from watching WWE. From phones and toys. I am from the loud TVs in my house. I am from the welcoming smell of my house. I am from the long grass and the large tree in my backyard.

I am from cookouts and party. From lots of cousins and yelling siblings. I'm from cooking and going out and from having fun.

I'm from trying my hardest and never giving up. And "Rise Up" by Andra Day. I'm from going outside. I'm from Brooklyn, NY, and America. Chicken and mac'n'cheese. Never giving up means to always get going. Even though it can be hard, you can overcome it.

I Am poem

by Shanice Jackson

I am broken and a fighter

I wonder if I should draw my thoughts away

I hear my grandma's voice

I see my sister waving

I want to be happy like my friends

I am broken and a fighter

I pretend to be normal

I feel happy in my dreams

I touch my sister's and grandma's hands

I worry every time I hear the words "bad news"

I cry every time I see my dad drinking

I am broken and a fighter

I understand that my life is worth fighting for

I say there is hope in life

I dream about me and my family not going through poverty

I try to draw my thoughts away

I hope happiness comes my way

I am broken and a fighter

Backstage

by Shanice Jackson

I am from electronics
from food and candles
I am from the smell of my dog and feeling safe
I am from the plants that sit at the window to get sun
The yellow flowers I see when I walk out the building

I'm from telling childhood stories and laughter
from siblings and cousins
I'm from eating and cleaning and from watching movies

I'm from never give up and have fun
and be better than me in life
I'm from celebrating simple things that make my parents
    happy

I'm from Brooklyn and I'm Puerto Rican and Black and eat
    rice and chicken all the time
From dancing with my grandma when music turns on
knowing that my grandpa is watching us with a smile on his
    face
seeing pictures on the wall and videos from when I was little
    and seeing everyone happy puts a smile on my face.

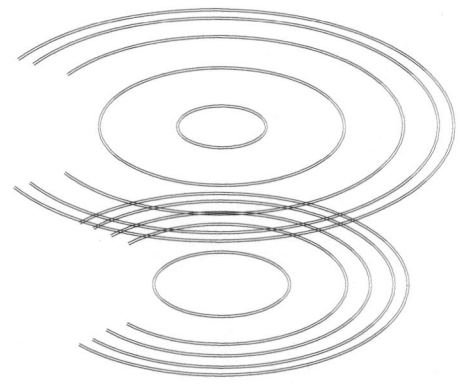

The Poisonous Snake~

by Aries Jones

I am pretty but poison
I wonder if I'll hurt more people
I hear a fan running
I see people that I like
I want the pain to stop

I am pretty but poison
I pretend that it's me and myself fighting
I feel sad
I taught my nephew how to draw
I worry about my family
I cry when it's too much on me

I am pretty but poison
I understand the pain that people feel
I say I'm OK
I dream that all the people's pain will stop
I try not to lie
I hope everything just stop
I am pretty but poison

I am poem

by Thomas Jones

I am Determination and Fearlessness
    I wonder if I will actually become a doctor when I grow up
        I hear Elmo laughing
            I see my grandfather sitting beside me
                I want I go to IHOP to get some pancakes

I am Determined and Fearless
    I pretend that I like people when I really don't
        I feel the sun hit my skin while I'm on the beach
        I touch my dream car
            I worry that high school is going to be hard
                I cry knowing that some kids don't have nowhere to sleep

I am Determined and Fearless
    I understand that sometimes things are not going to go my way
        I say nothing because I don't really like talking
            I dream that school is not annoying anymore
                I try to get sleep before school but can't
            I hope that I can get some sleep

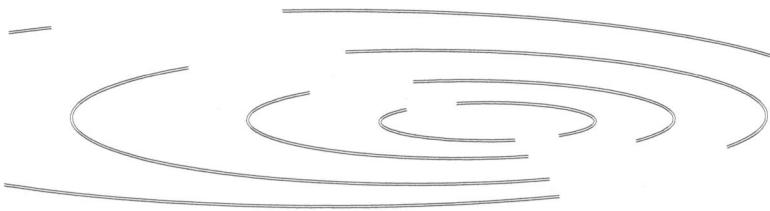

I am from poem
by Thomas Jones

I am from cleaning supplies

from phones and the TV

I am from the A apartment on the first floor

I am from the sunflowers and roses

the tree in front of my window

I'm from barbecue in the summer and game night every two months

from my sisters and my mom

I'm from running around the house and being on the phone most of the time

and from cooking for the whole family

I'm from "go to sleep, you have school tomorrow," and "you want to go to McDonalds?"

and "watch me whip, aye watch me nae nae"

I'm from eating at the table together

I'm from mac and cheese and chicken

I Am Poem
by Robert Kearney

I am smart
    I wonder about my future
        I hear voices in my head
            I see myself going to college
                I want to be taller

I am smart
    I pretend I'm fine sometimes when I'm not
        I feel pain
            I touch my controller for my game
                I cry for nothing really

I am smart
    I understand schoolwork
        I say I'm fine
            I dream for a good future
                I try to do my best for my mom
                    I hope that my sisters have a good life

I am smart

A Game of Chess with One Million Pieces on the Table

by Sherebiah Lawes

I am from waking up in the middle of the night like I am a nocturnal animal getting ready to start their day.

From crying under pillows and blankets so no one can see the hidden ocean I've created in my shirt.

From putting on an art show where all you see is my smiling face but when the museum closes the illusion fades to dust.

From a family of devoted Christians who go to church while they are suffering.

I'm from admiration and indulgence in the arts just to achieve the satisfaction of creating my own reality.

I'm from overeating and feeling dread and regret since I forget my own boundaries.

From losing my breath as my mind takes over my body and as it feels like I'm being dissected while my eyes are wide open.

I am from rumors becoming parts of who I am because fighting them off would just make more rumors.

I am from thinking of grotesque and anguishing actions but keeping my composure and reminding myself what I stand for.

From holding my passion, anguish, and all other emotions in a jar, locking that jar in a safe, and placing that safe in a place no one can reach, all to let it decay.

I'm from friends that taught me it's okay to be who I am or to be what I want to be.

From an amazing person who taught me how to feel freedom and love.

I'm from falling for people who will not reciprocate my feelings.

I am from having barely any friends and from accidentally causing them pain.

I am from feeling like I'm being dissected alive, fearful of what may come next.

But that's just life and maybe I am just a pawn in a game of chess with 1,000,000 pieces on the table and a few million tournaments to win and lose but I have to keep pushing or this game will never end.

Powerfully broken

by Sherebiah Lawes

I am powerfully broken

I wonder when my suffering will end because my own emotions are piercing me in the back

I hear the shouting and laughter of my friends and I sense the warmth of their hearts

I see a galaxy that seems safer than Earth, an empty void, dark and pristine, quiet and peaceful

I want to grow much stronger to protect my loved ones as if I'm the main character of a story

I am powerfully broken

I pretend nothing hurts me and put a mask on every day

I feel the love of characters that can't even love me to begin with

I touch their shoulders saying "I know how you feel." They say nothing back. That was to be expected

I worry that my fears will triumph over me for eternity

I cry when people get abused and hurt without reasoning

I am powerfully broken

I understand not everything goes as planned but it still irks me every day

I say "it's fine to not be fine." But the chances I apply that to myself are close to none

I dream my anxious and wary thoughts will come align like the stars or a lunar eclipse

I try to cover my emotional battle scars. "No one will know you're upset if you don't say anything"

I hope my friends won't leave me like my confidence left me when I was young

I am powerfully broken

What My Life Poem

by Malaki Lesser

Welcome readers my name is Malaki Lesser and I made a poem about who I am

I am strong and smart

I wonder if my future is going to be good

I hear my mom's voice

I see me having a good house and car

I want my grandpa back

I am strong and smart

I pretend I am a worker

I feel my mom's cold hands

I touched an elephant before

I worry about my moms

I cry for my grandpa back

I am strong and smart

I understand my mom's health is bad

I say it will get better

I dream for my dead family back

I try my best in school

I hope I pass in high school

I am strong and smart

My Goofy Poem
by Malaki Lesser

I am from P.S. 4

from juice and air

I am from the nice home that feels like my space

I am from the nice nature environment

The plants are nice and pretty in the spring

I'm from jokes and celebrations

from my mom and great-grandma

and from attitude

I'm from you better eat now

and watch my whip and ne ne

I'm from Palm Sunday

I'm from Long Island and Italian

pasta and sausage

From when my mom was sick because something was wrong with her head

My friend, my mom wasn't doing too good but she got better over time

I remember when we took a big family photo

That's So Diani
by Diani Lucas

I am independent and broken
I wonder what life has planned for me
I hear the sound of the fresh breeze singing in my ear like wind chimes in the air singing
I see my grandmother's beautiful soul in the sky telling me to never give up on what I love.
I want to be happy like the happiest kid on Earth getting candy
I am independent and broken

I pretend I'm a pretty princess who runs in a flower field escaping her castle with her charming prince.
I feel like a feather falling to the ground as it gives up on trying to fly away again
I touch my uncle's hand, hoping for some guidance to survive this cruel world
I worry about when it's my turn to leave this Earth for good or worse.
I cry because I'm not happy with what my life has turned into and how I grew as a person
I am independent and broken

I understand I mess up at certain points in life, it's a mistake I'm human
I say I promise to find my purpose in life and why I was brought on this earth
I dream about my success and wonder if it will ever work for me
I try to act okay when I'm not like parents on a Monday morning
I hope I'll be happy one day like the best man at his bro's wedding
But, I am independent and broken.

The Life of Ms. Lucas

by Diani Lucas

I am from messy clothes and sheets everywhere.
From getting yelled at to then getting spoiled.
I am from wooden floors to the smell of dinner cooking every night.
The lights flicker from my grandma as she gives us a sign she is always near
I'm from a great Thanksgiving and Christmas every year
From my mom's side to my dad's side.
I'm from celebrating my grandma's passing to crying about how she's gone too soon.

I'm from "Don't touch that, Diani" and "What do you wanna eat."
And "Good morning, Mr. Walker."
I'm from wearing the same shirts as my family.
I'm from Brooklyn and New York.

I'm from chicken and macaroni.
From seeing a ghost outside the glass window about how he had a hat and red glowing eyes.
From seeing ashes of my ancestors around my grandma's house.
I'm from hiding presents under my bed and lights and mirrors all around my wall.
I'm from the memory of my lost loved ones in my heart.

I Am Poem

by Jamel Mayo, Jr.

Stanza 1.
I am Jamel Mayo
I wonder why things always have to be difficult.
I hear a whole lot of lectures
I see a laptop
I want to do better in school
I am Jamel Mayo

Stanza 2.
I pretend that I will be successful
I feel like I'm never good enough for myself
I touch/scratch my head when I'm frustrated
I worry when it's too late to complete something
I cry when things are too overwhelming
I am Jamel Mayo

Stanza 3.
I understand when people are speaking to close my mouth and listen
I say things that a child my age isn't supposed to say
(Example) I say curse words like damn or sh*t and I know I'm not really allowed to say those words because I'm not grown and I need to stay in a teenager's place.
I dream of being successful
I try to do my best at making people proud but it's hard
I hope that things will get better for me and my grades
I am Jamel Mayo

Where I Am From

by Jamel Mayo, Jr.

I am from Brooklyn, New York. I am from art and music.

I am from projects where there are not any happy endings.

I am from the grass where it's hard to see things.

The trees near my house whose long gone limbs I remember as if they were my own.

I am from barbecues and mixed race from my mother and father.

I am from partying and sleeping and sometimes getting along.

I am from being the man in the house and being told "to try is to fail" and "life gets harder when you grow up."

I am Barbados and Puerto Rico.

I am from a family portrait located on my living room wall.

Happiness

by Schnieder Milien

I am playful and generous

I wonder if I can ever be a pro basketball player

I hear music every day

I see myself with a successful future

I want to have a fortune

I am playful and generous

I pretend I'm an adult sometimes

I feel determined most of the time

I touch my mother every day

I worry about my grades

I cry for the ones I lost

I am playful and generous

I understand that if you want something you have to go for it

I say I don't care

I dream of a successful future

I try to get classwork done

I hope we can go back to school

I am playful and generous

The World is an Unforgiving and Generous Place

by Leshaun Miller

I am strong and broken

I wonder if I can spend one more day with my aunt before she passed away from covid

I hear my grandfather talking right next to me trying to tell me something but I can't hear him

I wanted my aunt to be there for my football game but she didn't come but I stood strong and played the game

I want to see both of them alive again

I am strong and broken

I pretend I'm okay but I'm not

I feel my auntie hugging me

I touch my brother's face to tell him what happened and he started crying

I worry a lot about my family if they get into a car accident

I cried when my grandfather was in the hospital

I am strong and broken

I say everything is great people come and go to my mom and my whole family

I dream that my grandfather and aunt came back to life

I try not to think about my grandfather's death and my aunt's death

I hope my family stay safe

I am strong and broken

I am strong and broken

I wonder If I can spend one more day with my auntie

I hear my grandfather talking right next to me

I see my grandfather sitting down in the couch

I want to see both of them alive again

I am strong and broken

I understand that people died so I have to face that they are both gone

I say everything is great people come and go

I dream that my grandfather and aunt came back to life

I try not to think about my grandfather's death and my aunt's death

I hope my family stay safe

I am strong and broken

The place I belong

by Leshaun Miller

I am from basketball

from toothbrush and underwear

I am from the wood and chair

I am from the bee in a tree

I'm from a family party and football game

from my dad and my mom

I'm from my dad with his eating problem and my mom with her hair

I'm from Toy Story and Cat in the Hat and I don't know

I'm from Jamaica and Brooklyn

Fried chicken and burgers from my dad

because my dad likes to eat a lot of fried chicken but not that many burgers.

This is Me

by Dionyae Mitchell

I am happy and hurt

I wonder if I actually help anyone

I hear people laughing

I see a happy family

I want to be an artist

I am happy and hurt

I pretend I am famous

I feel my aunt hugging me

I touch her hands

I worry I will lose everything

I cry for things I can't control

I am happy and hurt

I understand I can't do everything

I say it will be ok

I dream for a day without pain

I try to keep a smile on my face

I hope my dreams come true

I am happy and hurt

The Birth of Me

by Dionyae Mitchell

I am from board games and baking tools.

From hair products and cell phones.

I am from the messy bedrooms, comfy sofas, and the smell of sweets in the kitchen.

I am from the pile of sneakers in the living room.

I'm from crazy party planning and family movie nights.

from a loving mother and a hardworking father.

I'm from forgetting tasks and random conversations.

and from unexpected screaming.

I'm from "babies are from babies r us" and "do you have McDonald's money?"

and "it's not impossible unless you try."

I'm from early planned family trips.

I'm from a hospital in Queens, Trinidad, sweet potato pie, and mac n' cheese.

From my mom flushing her cat and my uncle being bribed to help

I am from childhood sibling photos on my phone but also in my heart.

I Am from the Love of My Family

by Lillian Olivari

I am from the books
from the pen and paper
I am from the blank white walls with that one picture
The warmness and coldness
I am from the roses
The lilies in my mom's room

I'm from the baked mac and cheese every holiday and karaoke at every party
From my grandma and grandpa
I'm from the loud music and dancing
And from the cooking all day and the cooking all night

I'm from the look fear in the eyes and never let anyone bring you down
and "When the world seems so cruel and your heart makes you feel like a fool, I promise you will see I will be your remedy." My mother said the song reminded her of me
I'm from the sleepovers
I'm from Methodist Hospital and Brooklyn
Pork chops and mash potatoes
From the being a soldier in the war
The blue eyes and wavy hair
The big box of pictures of my aunt and uncles and their childhood
The pictures of my friends and family on my wall and the love I feel in my heart

I Am Who I Pretend to Be

by Lillian Olivari

I am friendly and enthusiastic

I wonder who I will be in the future

I hear the laughter of my friends when I tell a joke

I see the people dancing and singing at parties

I want everything to stay the same

But it didn't

I am now isolated from everyone and not only am I alone but I feel alone

I wonder when I will hear my friends' laughter once again

We lost contact and grew distant

I hear the silence from outside

I see the few people who walk down the streets with mask on

I want everything to get better, I want it all over

I now pretend I am happy

I feel emotionally drained and tired

Every day just feels like it repeats over and over again

I touch my computer getting ready for online school

Looking at a computer screen from 9:00 till 2:26 and then for the rest of the day doing the same as I did the other day before, nothing

I worry about if I will be able to actually go to high school and how I would talk to people

I cry because I don't know who I am anymore, I lost myself

I am now alone and afraid of what will happen next

Not only am I only alone but I feel alone and that is my biggest fear

I understand that this is serious and no one can help, people getting sick and dying

I say to my family how I feel and I am wrong for it

I dream the day I will finally go out

I try to keep my emotions to myself

I hope this will all get better

I am still figuring out who I want to be and what I am doing now, I just hope this all gets better

Positivity
by William Perez Jr.

I am positive and strong.
I wonder how my life will be when I grow up.
I hear my family talking.
I see my family having fun.
I want to get a PS5.
I am positive and strong.

I pretend I am Spider-Man.
I feel that I am cool which means I feel like I am a fun person to hang around with.
I touch my past family members.
I worry if I'm ok.
I cry when I am hurt.
I am positive and strong.

I understand that I have to go to school.
I say I will be fine.
I dream that I am Spider-Man because he is a superhero that has cool superpowers such as swinging on webs and crawling up walls which I wish I had. He also saves people and is my favorite superhero.
I try to do good in school.
I hope every day's a good day.
I am positive and strong.

I Am Family.

by William Perez Jr.

I am from TV, my cell phone and basketball. I am from the warmness and coziness of my home. I am from the bamboo plant that grows in my living room.

I'm from the breaking night on Christmas Eve and on the stroke of midnight, presents are opened on Christmas Day and the bravery from my mom and dad. I'm from picking up after myself and staying healthy and from getting good hours of sleep.

I'm from being told to behave good and respect others the way I would want to be respected and don't do to others what you don't want to be done to you. I'm from celebrating Thanksgiving with my family. I'm from Brooklyn NY and I'm Dominican and Puerto Rican. I'm from eating pizza and rice, beans and chicken. From my aunt who died before I was born, who as a kid grew up singing and had an opera voice. Who was understanding, and loved to tell jokes and was easy to talk to. A picture of her and my great grandmother together is hung up on my living room wall so I can see who they are.

Wish it, Want it, Do it

by Sa´Nye Seabrook

I am funny and smart.

I feel like a kid in a candy store.

I touch clouds.

I worry that if I leave home people will forget me.

I cry about nothing because I don't cry.

I am funny and smart.

I pretend like I don't care but I actually do.

I feel like a kid in a candy store. Seeing endless

I touch clouds.

I worry that if I leave home people will forget me.

I cry about nothing because I don't cry.

I am funny and smart.

I understand sometimes I just don't care.

I say stupid things sometimes.

I dream of having everything I could ever want.

I try to do different things but I like my way.

I hope that one day we will all be successful.

I am funny and smart.

The Truth Behind The Happiness.

by Sa´Nye Seabrook

I am from the TV remote and watching Saturday morning cartoons from the time the sun went up till when it went down and the couch.

I am from the 9th floor apartment and the feel of the hot air coming from the radiator.

I am from the heart of my mother. The strong tree with the leaves that flow in the wind.

I'm from having family movies and great fashion sense from brother to mother and sister.

I'm from singing and dancing while cooking and always asking questions while watching movies and from loving to watch Disney movies.

I'm from treating people how you want to be treated and NOOOO stop that's too much and Monster by Nicki Minaj.

I'm from wearing your pjs while opening gifts on Christmas.

I'm from Brookdale Hospital and New York and jerk chicken.

From my grandmother saving me from drowning in a pool to the same old paper trains and clay people me and family made.

The Beginning Of The End

by Nathaniel Stewart

I am unique and broken

I wonder what's my true purpose

I hear dogs barking

I see dead trees

I want everyone to be happy

I am unique and broken

I pretend that I'm happy

I feel like I have a purpose

I touch my mother's shoulder

I worry that I might lose my mom

I cry for the things I lose

I am unique and broken

I understand that I am something

I say I can help people be happy

I dream for everyone to be happy

I try to keep my friends from dying

I hope I don't lose anyone else

I am unique and broken

Behind The Skin

by Nathaniel Stewart

I am from my PS4 from the wooden doors and the closed windows.

I am from the quietest but loudest house that feels new and old.

I am from the trees outside. The trees whose long gone limbs I remember as if they were my own.

I'm from my grandma's memorial and drawings from my sister and my mother

I'm from staying up late and drinking coffee and from playing with my cat

I'm from wishing wells giving me good luck and from eating carrots will give me amazing eyesight and itsy bitsy spider

I'm from movie night

I'm from my hospital and Ireland or tacos and pork

From my great-x2 grandfather that fought in World War 2, about how he died and became a purple heart, pictures of me and my family that I treasure and mementos that are stored in my heart

I am Celina
by Celina Torruella

I am weird and talented

I wonder if life will change soon

I hear my shows I watch every day

I see my game on the tv

I want to be braver

I am weird and talented

I pretend my dog can understand what I say when I rant

I feel bored all the time

I worry I won't be able to do high school

I cry about everything

I am weird and talented

I understand that life can be difficult

I say everything is fine a lot

I dream about having a good future

I try to stay positive

I hope I accomplish things

I am weird and talented

I am from Home

by Celina Torruella

I am from my bed
From marshmallows and candy
I am from the apartment I call home
The home that I feel all my emotions
I am from the stuffed animal toy that I had since I was a baby
The roses I once received as a gift in this home

I'm from family events and hearing that same birthday song in Spanish every year
From grandpa and passed aunt
I'm from family drama and family make ups
And from seeing people happy one minute to breaking down the next

I'm from respect and always showing kindness
And "my little sunshine"
I'm from cookouts at grandpa's house
I'm from New York and a mixed family
Rice and chicken and quesadillas
From my parents growing up and making memories to tell me all about them
From the photo album
And the room in the back of my home
I am from my best friend and family

The Blessing In Disguise

by Kamani West

I am strong and gifted

I wonder if I am safe in the world we live in

I hear police sirens and ambulance sirens

I see homeless people left and right

I want to start my own business

I am strong and gifted

I pretend I am okay when sometimes I'm not

I feel homesick when I leave my family for too long

I touch my grandma's soft hands

I worry about my loved ones

I cry when I can't get something, for example my hair, or when I'm angry

I am strong and gifted

I understand things can't always go my way

I say don't worry Kamani there's always a blessing in disguise, meaning some things always happen in surprise just be patient

I dream to be on vacation in the Bahamas

I try to be the best I can be

I hope my dreams work out

I am strong and gifted

The Quiet Face Behind It All

by Kamani West

I am from a painting in a picture frame
From using utensils to ending up with dishes
from the home where it's very little quietness to extreme loudness
I am from meeting people for the first time til being quiet around them because I'm not used to them
I am from magic everywhere I walk something magical happens

I am from a home where Thanksgiving and Christmas is a family tradition
I am from a family where when you walk into someone's house you can smell the aroma of cornbread, chicken, rice, vegetables cooking on the stove top.
I am from a family where candles are always lit up to catch the aroma of the room
I am from a family that finds everything funny
I am from a family where everything they see has to be neat or clean
I am from a family who once told me to be a leader and not a follower

I am from a family where the song they always played for me was Let It Go by Elsa in the movie Frozen
I am from a family that always has family events
I am from a family where old school music is the only thing they love

Can You See Me

by Skyla W.

I am worried but Devoted

I think of the world as a battlefield

I wonder if I'm gonna make it through this harsh and cruel world

I hear everyone pushing me to be my best I never stop going

I see my goals sitting in front of me

I want to reach for all my goals

I am worried but Devoted

I pretend I'm in a different reality

I feel pressured to do my best

I touch my goals but never grab them

I worry I won't make it

I cry when I feel hurt

I am worried but Devoted

I understand I need to do what's right

I say I can but I don't

I dream to accomplish my goals

I try to achieve everyone's wishes

I hope to be the best

That's why

I am worried but Devoted

Can you see past the cover
by Skyla W.

I'm from the crown where royalty lives from my feet to my hair

I am from the white hard walls in my home to the bright sky that shines over me feels like stars fills up my head

I am from the fragile leaf that breaks off as time pass

I am from holiday joy and celebrations from family gatherings to gifts

I am from respect for adults and never talk back from "a harsh and cruel world"

I am from a well, wrapped town full of lights and joy on one specific night

I am from a hospital, a place with tall buildings and skyscrapers from bake and saltfish all year around

over my head on my slightly bare walls lie some frames hanging down with my closest family watching from above

I am from a place where I am safe a place where I am protected a place where I can call home

About the Authors

David Areche p. 8

Hi! My name is **David Areche** and what makes me is playing basketball. Playing basketball is something I love to do and enjoy. I wish that one day I'll have a spot in the NBA, that's a big goal I want to accomplish. Also, another thing that makes me is my family. My family makes me push harder everyday and I like to make them proud.

Tameyah Argudin p. 10

I am the "spends her family's money recklessly but spends her own money like she's a cheapskate" award-winning champ . . . jk ! **Tameyah Argudin** is the girl who is strong because she was able to overcome her past struggles with her perseverance and was able to get to a better place in her life. She admires her single mother because she was able to deal with all of her ups and downs without a male's support and she deeply appreciates and admires her for her independence. She says that home is her being around family, (including her pets), and wherever the wifi box is!

Ciara Ayala p. 14

What makes me is I dream big. I dream big means I want a lot of things in life. I wanna be an Entrepreneur, mother, famous, a billionaire, and much more. Also what makes me is that I'm from a big family. Family always comes before anyone and I say this because no matter what, family is always there for me so same for them. And if a famous person was to read this, this will be the way I want them to know me.

Ciara Camilus   p. 16

I'm Cece, well, no one besides my family actually calls me that. Of course there is a story to my nickname, a very simple story. On a standard sweltering Wednesday morning, sometime in the summer of 2007, I was born. Almost immediately after being brought home for everyone to behold the sight of the new addition to the family, my mother announced my name to the remainder of my family, "Ciara." My great grandmother struggled to pronounce my name, therefore I had been referred to as Cece. I think I've yet to properly introduce myself—Hi, I'm **Ciara Camilus.** Storytelling is something I deeply enjoy as well as reading and writing said stories. I live in the city of New York, also known as the city that never sleeps. And yes this is very much true, New York does not sleep. That's actually one of the many things I love about New York. No matter what time it is, there is always something going on. Some other things I love include myself haha, cats, the night time, very chill music, and anime. I have a huge obsession with anime to the point where I make watching anime my one and only personality trait. Anywho I hope you've gotten a sense of who I am now!

Chloe Campbell   p. 18

Hi my name is **Chloe Campbell** and I'm from NYC. I have lived 13 out of 200 years so far and I think I'm pretty smart for my age in certain areas. I'm always tired which might be a problem and I'm pretty sure it shows in this biography. Anyway, I wrote this poem because my hunger is everlasting like my laziness. Oh I forgot to say I'm in the eighth grade and going to high school pretty soon so if you see me in high school then hi! Ok bye.

Makayla Campbell p. 20

Hi my name is **Makayla Campbell** and I am 13 years old and my favorite color is royal purple. I am a very silly person. Something you would never know about me is that I'm allergic to cats but I really want a kitten but I'll probably sneeze to death. I love music in a way no one will ever understand. I will always love annoying my mom no matter how old I get. I feel like press conferences are very fake to make people feel sabotaged about being asked questions. I feel like no one should have to change what they look like in order to fit into today's beauty standard. We are all beautiful either dark skin, brown skin, or light skin and I just learned to believe that. We should all learn and know that there is no such thing as a perfect girl.

Arianna Crews p. 22

Hola como esta it's **Arianna Crews**, yes Crews not Cruz. Some people say that I'm fun to be around, some people know me as loud but energetic, and I guess I'll just say I'm just Arianna and what I mean by that is that I'm just myself, what I do, the way I act, my personality, my ways, I think it all makes me, Arianna. Also, my mother makes me who I am. She's been through a lot of risk and struggles with being a single parent but also loving, spoiling me, and supporting me through everything and anything.

Damaris Cruz p. 25

I am **Damaris Cruz**, a girl who enjoys doing makeup as much as she enjoys writing. I believe that I'm meant to do something great with my life, even though I don't know where to begin that great life. Someone who gives me the confidence and ability to think that is my uncle; he has always been like a father to me besides my actual dad, and he always takes care of everyone around him, including his many, many kids. He has always let me know that he has faith in me no matter what, and I will always tell him he can have

that faith all he wants, but don't ever ask me to babysit...
Im jp but for real don´t.

Akoni Drysdale-Ash p. 26

My name is **Akoni Drysdale-Ash**, I'm different and I wouldn't want to be human if there was another option. I can't really say what I am because I take an interest in multiple things. I play basketball in the hood and I'm the only female. When I'm picked on it makes me stronger and I don't mean in class. If there was an award for being the gayest in middle school I would win for sure. I love cookie dough ice cream, Stranger Things, short females, gay parades, gay books, Lil Nas X's Call Me By Your Name song, you ;) if you're a female, flirting and being able to be gayer than I am. But I'm a bit conceited. I like being the center of attention but long story short I'll be famous.

Jaynise Duval p. 29

My Name is **Jaynise Duval** and this is what makes me myself. I am a person who likes to do things in a certain way. I like to have things in order and if it's not in order, I have to fix it or it's gonna bother me. I like to match when I dress, even if it's casual. But if it's a quick thing to do, I will put on something comfortable. I am quiet when I first meet someone or new surroundings, but when I start to adjust to it, I'm less quiet and I interact more with people around me. I like to go outside and get some fresh air because I'm usually stuck in the house, but I try to get outside. I like to be around my family and friends because I rarely get to see my family, but I do talk to my best friends. What I like to do on my own time is be on my phone talking to my best friends, and since I am home most of the time, I like to stretch for my flexibility, just to move around and not stay in the same spot. I'm interested in self care, hair, beauty, and health.

Alexandra Flores

p. 30

*Oh! So you decided to look back here? Well since you have let me steal your attention for a couple of minutes! I'm **Alexandra Flores** but you can call me Alex. It's shorter although people might confuse me as a man but I'm not! I am actually a writer! Outside of what you're about to see I have written a few stories based off of more fantasy-based worlds because real life is like an endless hole and every day we are all falling deeper and deeper into it but let's look past our existential dread and let me tell you about my awards (because then I have a better chance of getting my book read). I mainly have basic school awards that a handful of kids get every marking period but other than that I have self proclaimed awards. For example, The Award for Reading Misspelled Messages! So welcome to whatever this is about to be!*

Licia Garcia

p. 32

*Hello, I am **Licia Garcia** and just will talk about my life here! As a kid, when I was a small child, I was rather interesting to people...but when I was young, I started to get into reading easily. So when I grew up more, I used to read and write anything I wanted. I made a few stories as a kid and showed it to friends. It was lovely...but when I got more into writing I wrote A TON OF WORDS that made many teachers that I had in English Language Arts or humanities impressed with my work. So I also started to write stories on Wattpad and not sure if they could read them. I either made up to 5,000 or to 8,000 words. Also, I've always wanted to write a lot more and show it to the world where they can be fascinated and touched by my lovely work and to make me famous to finally suck up my old self and to bring something personal into not-personal things. I want to make people happy with what I draw and write, so I do what I can to inspire people to be like me! If you want to or not, you can read it. Go ahead! If you don't like it, don't pick out something else. I don't care!*

Cassidy Grays-Ferguson   p. 34

My name is **Cassidy Grays-Ferguson**
I like to play sports, basketball, and rugby.
I am very funny and outgoing.
I have five siblings, one sister and four brothers. Two are twins; the boys are younger than me, and my sister is older.
I have two dogs. One is a girl and the other is a boy.

Sadeyah Harrison   p. 36

Hello, I am **Sadeyah (deyah) Harrison.** I am 14 years old and I live in New York City with my mother, father, and siblings. I am a very athletic outgoing person but can get annoyed quickly. I like to write and sometimes solve people's problems and give advice. I am reliable and a person you can always count on. I am my own inspiration and anything that's in my head I say or attempt to reach the goal. I always remember to be free.

Richelle Ashanti Horsford   p. 40

Hey, I'm **Richelle Ashanti Horsford** and I will make that known to you any chance I get. I very much have an I-could-care-less attitude. I might care but usually I don't or just don't show it. Ya don't need to know how I actually feel. I'm not sentimental. Don't fall in front of me or I'ma laugh. Like I laughed at my friend who fell off her skateboard—it was HILARIOUS. But other than my joy of laughter, I love celebrity drama, Madea, Rihanna, Star, Myself, pranking people, etc. I mean, I don't love celebrity drama but it's so interesting. I stay to myself a lot. My business isn't really your business. Like what I look like? As my best friend would say: "a pigeon." When I'm bored I occasionally cry, prank people, listen to music, play my game and bother my mother. But honestly, that's all you need to know. Goodbye.

Brianna Jackson

p. 43

I'm **Brianna Jackson** because of all the stuff I've been through. I'm the strongest person I know. Sometimes I might not act like it, but I'm very smart. I don't like to be told what to do. Family is everything to me. My friends are like my brothers and sisters and I will do anything for them. I have two sisters that are my blood and one that is my step sister, but I look at her as my blood. I have one blood brother. I love my sisters to death. My brother is very annoying, but I love him, I guess. Sometimes I let my anger get the best of me, but I'm working on that. I like to be alone and am not a "people person" at all. I like my space. I have a very good personality. I'm very shy at first, but once I warm up, I'm very fun. Sometimes I can be goofy. I like to laugh. I like fashion and I like animals. One day I hope to be a vet.

Khalik Johnson

p. 44

Khalik Johnson is an 8th grade student at Academy for Young Writers. I'm a member of Brooklyn, NY. I am a relaxed and calm person, but I am also a very shy person. I love to play sports and love to do science. My favorite animal is a dog. I like to eat food like pizza, hot wings, mac'n'cheese, yams, and salad. I like comedy and action movies like Ride Along 2 and Fast and Furious. They are funny and also have action in them. I liked to watch TV shows like Scooby-Doo and The Amazing World of Gumball. I like to play games a little bit on the weekends and focus on school during the weekdays. I am looking forward to 9th grade.

Shanice Jackson

p. 46

Hey, I am **Shanice Jackson.** I am music, music helps me express myself. It really brings out the good in me and that's what I love. I am adventurous, I like to explore the wildlife. It could be camping, hiking, or anything that has to do with wildlife. I feel like it's good to experience or try new things and have fun. I am a drawer, drawing brings me peace. It's another way of expressing myself and drawing is something that a lot of people don't really know that I like to do. Whenever I need to calm down I draw, when I'm bored I draw, it really doesn't matter how I'm feeling it's just something I like to do. I am social, I love making friends / meeting people. It puts a smile on my face knowing that I can have people to talk to or hang out with but I always keep my circle small. I am joyful, I love being happy. I hate knowing or seeing myself sad because that's not how I want to be. I'm the type of person to act silly around people all the time or people seeing me with a smile on my face that's what brings me joy. This is what makes me...Me.

Aries Jones p. 49

(**Aries Jones** doesn't write bios.)

Thomas Jones p. 50

I'm **Thomas Jones** and this is my bio. I feel like I am a kind person even though my friends say that I'm mean. Sometimes things come out as mean, but they're not, I promise. I like to be myself and try new things (which is really hard for me) because trying new things is not me. My favorite subject in school is science because to me it's really interesting and it's a class I never fall asleep in (unless I'm REALLY tired).

Robert Kearney p. 53

My name is **Robert Kearney**. I was born in New York City. I am Hispanic and African-American. My age as of today is 13 years old. I am in the Academy for Young Writers. In 6th grade I won my advisory's spelling bee and I was in the honor society. I will be going to Academy For Young Writers for high school and hope to continue achieving my goals and dreams.

Sherebiah Lawes   p. 54

My name is **Sherebiah Lawes** (or that's part of it since I actually have five names all together). I love writing, art, anime, K-pop, J-pop, and probably an assortment of other things as well. I'm the most optimistic pessimist you could possibly meet. I'm pretty good at lying (that's not exactly a good thing but whatever). I always get A's somehow which is surprising to me since I never focus in class. I can't run for the life of me and if I tried I would have to take out my asthma pump (I don't have asthma, I just forget how to breathe and it helps me). If you say something bad about me and I actually feel bad about it, that means I care about you and you should be honored (that sounds like I'm a narcissistic piece of trash but trust me, I'm quite the opposite). I have been writing a lot for a few years, I guess. My teachers all want me to write a book or something so that's fun even though I would probably have a mini heart attack since I have the lowest self-esteem possible. I'm that person that says "oh I'll do great" even though on the inside I'm doubting myself. Anyways, you guys want to go buy some ramen? No? Alright, fine! I see how it is! Bye then you.....you.....unkind human? You know what, bye.

Malaki Lesser   p. 58

The things that make me feel me is that I'm like a home person because I just stay home and play video games with my friends. Another thing that makes me feel myself is I don't let people push me around and I just don't mind it because I don't let people do that to me. The thing that I don't like about mean people is that they bully you but they try to act tough in front of their friends. My accomplishments are getting life going, getting a house and a car, and taking care of my mom.

Diani Lucas
p. 60

My name is **Diani Lucas**. Just remember, better days will come. I'm the independent woman you can't mess with. I am the most bomb female in the world in my head. I am God; she is me; God is a woman, and I am she.

Jamel Mayo, Jr.
p. 62

Hello my name is **Jamel Mayo, Jr.** and I was born on July 11, 2007. I was raised in Brooklyn, New York in Pink Houses projects. I went to Public School 224 and I graduated. I am interested in art and sketch because it helps me relax or helps me be entertained whenever I am bored. I want to publish my art in a museum that I want to invest in.

Schnieder Milien
p. 65

What makes me "me" is my determination and when I really want to do something I guess I get it done. Like this work right now: I didn't want to really do this work but now I put my mind to it and now I'm finishing it. If everyone in the world was to read this, I would want them to know me as carefree.

Leshaun Miller
p. 66

Hey my name Is **Leshaun Miller**. I like playing games and playing basketball but sometimes playing football. My favorite food is pizza (Domino's), chopped cheese, and my mom's home cooked fried chicken. The thing I don't like is when two people are talking to me at once. I won a lot of trophies, for example: I got a football trophy and a basketball trophy and I never really thought I would have any karate medals but I have two. I'm from Jamaica and America but I was born in Jamaica. I love to travel with my family.

Dionyae Mitchell   p. 70

Hi, my name is **Dionyae Mitchell**. I am fourteen years old, and I'm about to go to high school. I am an artist, and my goal is to grow in my artworks and become a graphic designer. Some of my greatest achievements were when I had gotten through the problems and complications of applying to art schools. Another one of my achievements was winning the whole school science fair. I feel what makes me strong is knowing that I have younger siblings who look up to me and how much of a role model I am to them.

Lillian Olivari   p. 72

My name is **Lillian Olivari**, but you can call me Lily for short. When I get older I dream to be a CSI. A lot of people get afraid of murders and all of that stuff. But to me it excites me, and it is something I am really considering doing. I want to be an independent woman and go to school for as long as it takes. I love music; no matter what genre or emotions it makes me feel, I will always love it. I also love writing. While I write, I listen to music, or even while I do anything, I listen to music. It puts me in the mood. I have a little brother whom I love a lot. I will do anything for him. I also have a dog, and he is my best friend. My biggest accomplishment has to be getting all As in school. I love when I get my report card and see my grades; it makes me feel so proud of myself knowing that I did it. My favorite thing in the world is to spend time with my friends. I always use the quote, "You only live once; you die in the end anyways." It makes me want to live life and just do it. I also like to go outside and ride my skateboard. The fresh air always puts me in a good mood. I feel sort of free, you could say, like I have no worries. It makes me feel as if I am in a movie, and I am the main character. But that is who I am, but there are so many other things about me that are so much more interesting.

William Perez, Jr.   p. 76

Hi everyone. My name is **William Perez Jr.** and I'm from Brooklyn. I like to spend time with family, watch YouTube, TV, Netflix and play video games such as Fortnite, Marvel's Avengers, Spider-Man, Gang Beast, Brawlhalla, NBA2k20, etc. I also like going to amusement parks. I am an athletic person who likes to play basketball. I hope to be in the NBA or be a YouTube content creator.

Sa´Nye Seabrook   p. 78

Hi, I am **Sa´Nye Seabrook**. I am a fun-loving kid who likes cartoon shows from throughout all the ages. I'm a person who thinks homework should be illegal and the same person who thinks if it wasn't on YouTube then it must not be real. I am a person who would love to get the opportunity to just sit and play video games all day. I would take it. I'm the person who could take a joke and the same person who can make them. I am the person who broke their TV with a PENNY. I am the person who forgets to leave the house with a mask. But I think that's what makes me real and what makes me ME, I also find that with these traits and mistakes it makes me unique and makes everyone unique in their own way.

Nathaniel Stewart   p. 80

Hi. My name is **Nathaniel Stewart**. I'm from Brooklyn and I'm 16 years old. I would say one word that sums up my life is catastrophic, but sometimes my life can be good. It's like a switch up. If i'm being honest it's hard for me to find a place that feels home to me other than my own home. I will say that it's not really a place but a person that feels like home. For example, how people care about me or how they help me. Personally, I feel like I could win an award for sarcasm because, trust me, I can be really sarcastic if I don't really like someone. But, it's kinda rare for me to not like someone. This might sound crazy but most of the time pain makes me stronger. Now I'm not talking about physical pain; I'm talking about mental pain. For example, breaking up, or even losing someone. They make me stronger most of the time just as one of my favorite quotes says, "Pain makes me grow. Growing is what I want. Therefore, for me pain is pleasure." -- Arnold Schwarzenegger

Celina Torruella p. 82

I'm **Celina Torruella** and I'm a 13 year old girl with a couple dreams I wish to accomplish. I don't know how to explain myself but I'll explain by saying what I like. Cars: I want a nice sports car. Sports: I love sports—watching them and playing. My favorite is basketball. Anime: I love it, watch it on a daily basis. I'm not a girly girl type so I dislike all of that. I don't care much about what people think of me. I just chill and do my own thing. I'm not much of an electronics person with phones and iPads and stuff unless I'm watching something. I used to be though. But I learned that I dislike social media and so I removed it. Now I'm just a girl who plays video games, watches anime, and stays in bed all day hoping I will become something good in life.

Kamani West p. 84

Hey guys I'm **Mani** but no one really calls me that besides my family, but beside that what makes me me is my vibe is immaculate. I'm a person you would want to invite anywhere because I'm good vibes. I always bring good energy instead of negative energy. I have a love for seafood. My sign is a Pisces which means we can be very loving and caring but for a Pisces I don't fit that category. Let's talk about me: sometimes I struggle with understanding my friends. When I don't get their point of view it makes things hard because they just think I'm trying to start an argument for no reason when that's not the case. Most nights I'm upset because I get overwhelmed and start to think about negative things and that would get me upset but then I just push it to the side and forget about it. Overall I just want to start things off fresh with a new life, I mean everyone needs to start all over again once in a while.

Skyla W.

*My name is **Skyla W.** I'm pretty sure you don't know who I am. Well I don't really know either. Get this, I have never written a real poem before so it's kinda weird but exciting. I'm not really a shy person so my words might be quite blunt. I just don't speak up as much as I should. Well, I guess I'm in eighth grade and thirteen years old but for some reason I think of my future more than the present which is weird because the present makes the future. As you read, it's best if you read between the lines. In my poem, I state who I am and where I'm from. I'm not the type of person to share my feelings or let people get to know ME. But, as I said, I need to speak up more so here's me.*

Acknowledgments

In our Young Writers Publish program, 826NYC works with classes of students and teachers on creative writing projects around and beyond New York City. Eighth grade students from the Academy for Young Writers explored poems about self and identity this year to produce the beautifully original and detailed poetry in this book. *No One Can See the Hidden Ocean I've Created* is a compilation of the original work of these students.

A huge thank you to our 826NYC teaching artist, Willie Filkowski, for creating a virtual classroom where students could revisit and reimagine their work, and write about themselves as writers. Your support, encouragement, and consistency helped our young authors tap into their imaginations and memories to produce such moving work, and your care in this process was invaluable.

We are particularly grateful to Henya La Noue and Deborah Barton for their support of this project. Thank you for diving head first into this publication, bringing with you months of incredible lesson planning, close readings, and innovative writing classes. Your hard work and steadfast dedication to your students and their creative vision allows them to flourish as young writers and thinkers.

At 826NYC we depend on the dedicated volunteer editing and design cohort that make our publications a reality. Thank you to Joe Iovino and Anthony Iovino for designing such a beautiful book for our students. To copy editors and proofreaders Melissa Feinman, Jen Ha, Michelle Haska, Amy Linstrom, Christine Marella,

Lauren Pruitt, Allison Singer, and Rachel Spurrier for their careful attention to each of the student's pieces, thank you.

A big thank you to The Jane Friedman Anspach Family Foundation, The Hawkins Foundation, The Rona Jaffe Foundation, The Kettering Foundation, The Minerva Foundation, The Pinkerton Foundation, and The Resnick Family Foundation, the New York City Department of Cultural Affairs in partnership with the City Council, and the National Endowment for the Arts, for their generous support, which allows us to publish our students' work. The program is also made possible by the New York State Council on the Arts with the support of Governor Andrew M. Cuomo and the New York State Legislature.

Thank you especially to the 826NYC staff for their behind-the-scenes support of this project, from curriculum development and the book-making process to volunteer recruitment.

Finally, thank you to the students at the Academy for Young Writers for taking risks with your writing and sharing your words with us. Writing can be a challenging and hopefully fun process, and your dedication to your craft and sharing these incredibly special pieces of yourselves shines through in these poems. We are all excited to see what books you'll produce in the future!

About 826NYC

826NYC Location and Leadership

826NYC and The Brooklyn Superhero Supply Co.
372 Fifth Ave
Brooklyn, NY 11215
718.499.9884
www.826nyc.org

Staff

Joshua Mandelbaum, Executive Director
Naomi Solomon, Director of Education
Corey Ruzicano, Programs Coordinator
Summer Medina, Community Engagement Strategist
Jesusdaniel Barba, Programs Coordinator
Lauren Everett, Communication & Fundraising Coordinator
Chris Eckert, Store Manager

Board of Directors

Michelle McGovern, President
Ted Wolff, Vice President
Ray Carpenter, Treasurer
Kathryn Yontef, Secretary
Michael Colagiovanni
Jen D'Ambroise
Liza Demby
Jamal Edwards
Amir Mokari
Arjun Nagappan
Tammy Oler
Katie Schwab
Danielle Sinay
Andrew Sparkler
Alyson Stone
Maura Tierney
Thom Unterburger

826NYC Programs

Write After School

Reading and writing go together like peanut butter and jelly. Write After School students work alongside 826NYC staff and volunteers to build their reading, writing, social-emotional skills and unleash their imagination as they play and learn about the power of language. Three times a year, students revise their creative writing for publications that are printed in English and Spanish and shared with families, volunteers, and community members at celebratory readings.

Write Away Workshops

Young writers come together in Write Away Workshops to explore a multitude of genres and subjects and to develop their voices. Groups write freely and participate in imaginative writing activities and lessons. Whether it's a song, a piece of climate justice sci-fi, or a nature guide, young writers leave the workshop with a piece to be proud of, as well as a newfound understanding of the topic, and new friends.

Young Writers Publish

Turn your classroom into a creative writing lab. During Young Writers Publish residencies, 826NYC teaching artists collaborate with educators on creative, impactful, curriculum-aligned projects that transform students into published authors. Residencies run from six weeks to a full year, depending on the project. Each Young Writers Publish culminates in a book, newspaper, zine, podcast, film, or performance featuring your students.

Write Together

826NYC hosts classes across New York City for Write Together: an interactive writing experience that encourages creative expression, explores the elements of storytelling, and strengthens writing skills. Elementary-aged classes collaborate on illustrated children's books, middle schoolers choose their own adventure, and high schoolers learn the art of memoir writing during a fast- paced and whimsical 90 minute narrative program.

Teen Writers Collective

Teens are the next generation of literary leaders. That's why we launched the Teen Writers' Collective. The collective brings together young writers from around the city to explore the art of writing and literary citizenship. They are a community of passionate and creative peers, serve as 826NYC youth leaders, and inspire younger students and peers across the network.

Student Publications

Through our programs, our volunteers work with students to help them create stories, poems, and 'zines. Because we believe that the quality of students' work is greatly enhanced when they are given the chance to share it with an authentic audience, we are committed to publishing student works. By encouraging their work and by guiding them through the process of publication, we make abundantly clear that their ideas are valued.